DiG iT: HiSTORY FROM OBJECTS

The Egyptians

John Malam

PowerKiDS press™

New York

Published in 2011 by The Rosen Publishing Group Inc.
29 East 21st Street, New York, NY 10010

Copyright © 2011 Wayland/
The Rosen Publishing Group, Inc.

First Edition

Produced for Wayland by Calcium
Design: Paul Myerscough
Editor: Sarah Eason
Editor for Wayland: Camilla Lloyd
Illustrations: Geoff Ward
Picture Research: Maria Joannou
Consultant: John Malam

Library of Congress Cataloging-in-Publication Data

Malam, John, 1957-
  The Egyptians / by John Malam. — 1st ed.
      p. cm. — (Dig it: history from objects)
  ISBN 978-1-4488-3283-5 (library binding)
  1. Egypt—Civilization—To 332 B.C.—Juvenile literature. 2. Egypt—Antiquities—
Juvenile literature. I. Title.
  DT61.M284 2011
  932—dc22

                                        2010023834

Photographs:
Corbis: The Gallery Collection 11t, Sandro Vannini 23; Dreamstime: Asier
Villafranca 17b; Fotolia: Cambo 6, Sam Shapiro 4, 20b, Sootra 15t; Shutterstock:
Bestimagesever.com 9t, 19b, Zbynek Burival 15b, 26b, CROM 18, Louise Cukrov
25t, Erkki & Hanna 19t, 22b, 26t, Fatih Kocyildir 17t, Nagib 22t, Jennifer Leigh
Selig 20t, Ian Stewart 5, 16, Tkachuk 13t, 26c; Topham Picturepoint: 8, 9b; Wayland
Picture Library: 21, 25b, 27b; Wikimedia: 3, 24, Cyberjunkie 14, Loïc Evanno 7,
27t, Marie-Lan Nguyen 13b, Andreas Praefcke 10, The Yorck Project/Zenodot
Verlagsgesellschaft mbH: 11b, 12, 27c. Cover photograph: Shutterstock: Tkachuk

Manufactured in China
CPSIA Compliance Information: Batch #WAW1102PK: For Further Information
contact Rosen Publishing, New York, New York at 1-800-237-9932

Contents

Who Were the Egyptians?   6

Homes and Towns   8

Farming and Food   10

Clothes and Crafts   12

Pharaohs   14

Pyramids and Other Tombs   16

Gods and Temples   18

Mummies   20

The Egyptians at War   22

Writing   24

Quiz   26

Timeline   28

Glossary   29

Further Information and Index   30

Who Were the Egyptians?

The Egyptians lived on the **fertile** banks of the Nile River for more than 3,000 years. The Nile River flows through Africa to the Mediterranean Sea. The ancient Egyptians learned how to farm the land around the Nile and grew many crops.

Egypt, the Black Land

In ancient Egyptian times, the Nile burst its banks and flooded the land around it every year. When the flood ended, the land along the river's edge was left covered in black mud. The mud was fertile and perfect for farming, which is why people lived along the edge of the river. The ancient Egyptians called their homeland Kemet, which means "Black Land," after the mud.

NO MORE FLOODING

In 1971, the Aswan High Dam was built. It contains water from the Nile River to make a huge reservoir. As a result, the Nile River no longer floods Egypt.

Two Kingdoms

At the start of ancient Egyptian history, Egypt was divided into two kingdoms. The kingdom in the north was called Lower Egypt and the kingdom in the south was called Upper Egypt. Around 3100 BCE, a king named Narmer united the two kingdoms. From then on, Egypt became one land, ruled by kings called pharaohs.

The Nile River flows the entire length of Egypt.

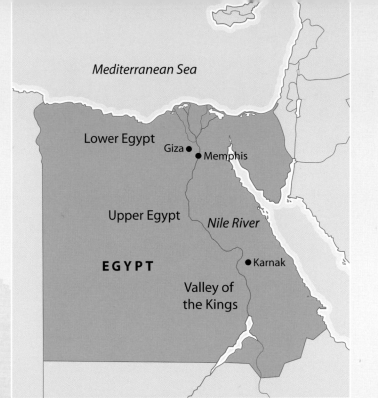

Mediterranean Sea

Lower Egypt
Giza ● ● Memphis

Upper Egypt   *Nile River*

EGYPT   ● Karnak

Valley of the Kings

What Does it Tell Us?

This is a model of a boat used by the Egyptians to sail on the Nile River. Boats such as this one carried people, **goods**, and animals across Egypt. When boats sailed south along the river, they sailed against the **current**. The boats then used a sail, which caught the wind to help them move forward against the current. When boats sailed north along the river, the current carried them forward. A man at the back of the boat steered using a long piece of wood called a tiller.

Homes and Towns

Ancient Egyptian towns and cities, including the **capital**, often grew up around a big **temple** or palace that belonged to the pharaoh. Towns were made up of many winding streets, filled with houses. Workshops also lined the streets. In them, craftsmen made goods such as pots, fabric, and furniture.

Houses of Mud

The poorest Egyptians lived in small, one-roomed houses made of **mud brick**. They were painted white to reflect the Sun's heat. This kept the house cool. Mud brick crumbles easily, which is why there are no ruins of Egyptian houses today. Houses were also made of reeds or sticks covered with mud.

What Does it Tell Us?

This is a model of an ancient Egyptian town house. Around 500 BCE, tall houses such as this one became fashionable. The houses were made of mud brick, and could be two or three stories high. The ground floor was often a workshop, in which the owner worked. Above that were the living rooms, in which people cooked and slept. The top floor was used to store the family's food.

Mud bricks were light and easy to build with. Builders stuck them together with watery clay mixed with sand.

MEMPHIS

Memphis was ancient Egypt's capital city for thousands of years. The main palace for the king was here, along with many temples.

Rich and Poor

The houses of poor Egyptians had very little furniture, often only a mud-brick bed to sleep on and some wooden stools to sit on. Rich Egyptians, such as **nobles** and the royal family, lived in big houses. They had many rooms, a garden, and a courtyard. Rich people had servants who lived with them. The houses also had rooms for visitors.

Only the richest Egyptians had pieces of furniture like this wooden chest.

Farming and Food

Most ordinary Egyptians were farmers who lived and worked on the fertile land along the Nile River. They began farming in mid-June. It was then that the Nile River began to flood, washing mud across the land. By October, the flood was over. Farmers then started to sow their fields.

Growing Crops

Farmers made small fields in the layer of fresh mud that covered the land after the flood. They planted emmer (a type of wheat) and barley. Emmer was the main food eaten by the Egyptians.

Farmers also grew onions, leeks, garlic, peas, lentils, beans, radishes, cabbages, cucumbers, and lettuces. Many fruits were grown, including grapes, figs, dates, and pomegranates. Flax was also grown. The plant's fibers were spun into **linen**, which was used to make clothes.

This model of a bakery shows workers grinding grain to make flour.

SANDY BREAD
Desert winds constantly blew sand toward the Nile River. The sand fell into dough, so people got used to gritty bread!

Farm Animals

The most important farm animal was the cow. Cows provided milk and meat. They also pulled carts and plows. Sheep and goats were also kept on Egyptian farms. They provided milk, meat, wool, and hides. Other animals kept for food were antelopes, gazelles, pigs, geese, ducks, and hens.

This wall painting shows farmers cutting grain crops.

On the Menu

What people ate in ancient Egypt depended on how rich or poor they were. Poor people ate bread, a few vegetables, fruit, and barley beer (a thick soup). They also hunted hares, fish, and wild birds for meat. Only the rich ate red meat from cows, or drank wine. These were luxuries.

What Does it Tell Us?

This is a wall painting of a farming scene in ancient Egypt. It shows a group of men harvesting emmer. The men are using cattle to help them harvest the crop. The painting shows us how important cattle were to the Egyptians as farm animals.

11

Clothes and Crafts

It is very hot in Egypt, so people wore simple, light clothes to keep cool. We know about the Egyptians' clothes from the models and statues that they made. Beautiful wall paintings also tell us what people looked like. We can tell that the Egyptians were skilled craftspeople from the objects that they left behind, such as pieces of jewelry and furniture.

This wall painting shows a woman wearing a wig, earrings, and a headdress.

Clothes and Footwear

Men wore loincloths (clothing a little like underpants) and women wore dresses. Clothes were usually white, but some were dyed red, blue, or yellow. Most clothes were made from linen. People wore sandals made from palm leaves and **rushes**, or walked barefoot. Sandals made of leather were very expensive. Only rich people wore these.

Hair and Hairstyles

Both men and women liked to wear wigs, which were made from human hair. Men wore short wigs, women had longer ones. Young boys had their heads shaved, except for one long piece, called a "sidelock of youth," This showed that the boy was still a child.

EYELINER

It was fashionable for both men and women to paint black makeup around their eyes.

12

What Does it Tell Us?

This famous bust is of Queen Nefertiti. Her name meant "beautiful woman," and the artist has shown this by making her very attractive. Nefertiti was the favorite wife of the great Egyptian king, Akhenaten. Nefertiti is shown wearing a tall hat and a wide necklace made from beads. Her eyes are lined with black makeup and she is wearing red lipstick.

Pieces of colored stone and glass have been used to make this jewel.

Ancient Crafts

The ancient Egyptians had many different crafts. **Stonemasons** made statues of gods and kings, and artists painted scenes on the walls inside tombs. These were burial places for important Egyptians such as kings and nobles. Jewellers worked with **precious metals** and rare stones, from which beads and lucky charms were made.

Pharaohs

Ancient Egypt was ruled by powerful kings called pharaohs. Most pharaohs were men, but Egypt was sometimes led by a woman pharaoh. The ancient Egyptians believed that the pharaoh was a god-king. This meant that he or she was half king and half god. Pharaohs were all-powerful and had the power of life and death over their people.

Ultimate Power

The ancient Egyptians had a **government** and an army. The pharaoh was in charge of both. It was also the pharaoh's job to bring good harvests. As a god-king, he was expected to use his superhuman powers to control the Nile River and make sure that it flooded every year.

Pharaohs were also shown as part lion and part human. This was an imaginary creature called a sphinx.

Helping to Rule

The pharaoh did not rule Egypt on his own. He had thousands of people who helped him. They were called officials and did the daily work of running the country. The most important official was called a vizier. He was the pharaoh's most trusted helper, and told him what was happening in the country.

SIGN OF GREATNESS
Pharaohs wore false beards tied to their chins with cords. A beard was a sign that the pharaoh was half god.

Royal Wives and Children

Egyptian pharaohs could have many wives, but only one queen. Pharaohs could have children with all their wives, but only the children of the queen were allowed to become pharaohs themselves. To become a pharaoh, a royal son had to marry a royal princess. That is why royal brothers were often married to their sisters.

Hatshepsut was a female pharaoh. She wore a false beard, just like male pharaohs.

What Does it Tell Us?

When pharaohs died, their bodies were **mummified**. This is the death mask of Pharaoh Tutankhamun. It was placed over the head of his mummified body. It is made from solid gold and semiprecious stones. Gold was used because it did not rot or lose its sparkle. The Egyptians believed the gods had flesh made of gold.

Pyramids and Other Tombs

Ancient Egypt's first pharaohs were buried inside tombs called pyramids. Pharaohs who ruled later were buried in tombs under the ground. Tombs were built to be safe places for the dead kings to rest in, but robbers broke into them. The robbers were looking for the many wonderful treasures often buried with the pharaoh.

Traveling to Heaven

The Egyptians believed pyramids joined Earth with heaven. That is why they were built for pharaohs. It was believed that after death, the pharaoh could travel straight to heaven from the pyramid.

What Does it Tell Us?

The Step Pyramid was Egypt's first pyramid. It was built for the pharaoh Djoser in the shape of a hill with six huge steps. Within 100 years of the Step Pyramid, builders could make pyramids with perfectly smooth sides, like those at Giza.

Pyramids at Giza

The most famous pyramids were built at Giza. Three huge pyramids stand here. They were built for the pharaohs Khufu, Khafre, and Menkaure who were father, son, and grandson. The pyramid of Khufu is known as the Great Pyramid. It was made from about 2.3 million blocks of stone and took 23 years to build.

The three pyramids at Giza belong to Menkaure, Khafre, and Khufu. The biggest pyramid at the center of this photograph belongs to Khufu.

Tomb Robbers

Tomb robbing was a problem in ancient Egypt. A solution had to be found, and so a new type of tomb was built. A valley far away from towns was chosen, where tombs were dug into the sides of the cliffs. It was called the Valley of the Kings. Even though the entrances to the tombs were hidden, robbers still figured out where to dig.

This wooden coffin is painted with gold and pictures of Egyptian gods.

DEAD GUILTY
The penalty for anyone caught robbing a tomb was death. The robber was impaled on a wooden spike and left out in the Sun.

Gods and Temples

The ancient Egyptians believed in hundreds of gods. Some were **worshiped** by a few people, others were worshiped by everyone. The Egyptians believed the gods controlled them completely. They had a god for every part of their lives, from farming and food, to reading and writing.

Home for a God

Egyptian gods were well cared for! Temples were built especially for them. These temples were believed to be their homes on Earth. Within each temple was a holy room. This was a small, dark place with a raised floor. A sacred statue of the god was placed here. On festival days, the Egyptians took the statue outside so that ordinary people could see the statue of the god and worship it.

What Does it Tell Us?

An obelisk was a tall, stone pillar that was placed in front of a temple. It was shaped to look like a mini-pyramid and was covered in gold. The obelisk was designed to look like a ray of sunshine. That reminded ancient Egyptians of their chief god Re, the sun god.

The Gods' Servants

Priests and priestesses who lived at the temples served the gods. Priestesses would play music and dance for the god statue. Priests performed **ceremonies**. Priests washed and dressed the god statue three times a day. They also gave it food. They did this to make the statue an attractive place for the god to live.

*Horus was shown as a god with the head of a falcon, a bird of **prey**.*

The Major Gods

Amun Ra	King of the gods
Aten	God of daylight and warmth
Anubis	God of embalming
Bastet	Goddess of joy and the home
Horus	God of the sky
Isis	Goddess of fertility and nature
Osiris	God of the afterlife and the dead
Re	God of creation, the sun god
Seth	God of chaos, storms, and evil
Thoth	God of wisdom, writing, reading, and mathematics

Statues of Horus show him as a falcon wearing the crowns of Upper and Lower Egypt.

Mummies

The Egyptians **preserved** the bodies of dead people and some animals. This is called mummification. The ancient Egyptians believed that after they died, they went to a world called the afterlife where they lived for ever. They believed they could only do this if their bodies were mummified.

Making a Mummy

It took about 70 days for a dead body to be made into a **mummy**. People who made a mummy were

Royal or noble children were also mummified.

called embalmers. They first took out the dead person's lungs, liver, **intestines**, and stomach. These organs were kept. The brain was pulled out through the nose and thrown away. The Egyptians believed it was of no use. The heart and the kidneys were left inside the body. Then the body was covered with natron (salty crystals). The natron slowly sucked all the liquid out of the body, until it was completely dry.

This is the mummy of a cat. Its face has been painted on the linen wrappings.

Wrapping and Burying

Once the body was dry, the embalmers prepared it for burial. They made the body look lifelike again by filling the empty abdomen with rags, sawdust, and even mud. The skin was oiled, the face was painted with makeup, and a wig was put on the head. Last of all, the body was then wrapped head-to-toe in strips of linen, then put in a coffin. The mummy was ready to be buried.

HAVE A HEART

The heart was left inside the body because it was thought to control intelligence and emotions. The person would therefore need it in the afterlife.

What Does it Tell Us?

The lungs, liver, intestines, and stomach of a dead body were dried with natron. They were then wrapped in linen strips and packed into four vases called **canopic jars**. Each jar had an image of the god who protected the organ inside.

Imseti protected the liver

Hapi protected the lungs

Duamutef protected the stomach

Quebehsenuef protected intestines

The Egyptians at War

It was the pharaoh's duty to protect Egypt from any enemies. Some pharaohs were warriors who built up and led great armies. These kings expanded Egypt by invading lands to the northeast of Egypt. The Egyptians invaded countries as far away as Turkey, creating a great empire that they ruled.

This wall painting shows a pharaoh firing arrows from a chariot. He is wearing a blue crown, or war crown.

What Does it Tell Us?

Pictures on the walls of tombs show Egyptian soldiers. Here, a group of men are shown setting off to war. The man at the front is armed with a throw stick. This was a heavy stick that could knock someone out. Behind him are men with spears and axes. They all have shields.

Army Fighters

The pharaoh's army was made up of foot soldiers, archers, and charioteers. Foot soldiers fought on foot with spears, axes, swords, and daggers. Archers fired sharp arrows at the enemy from a distance. Charioteers drove chariots pulled by horses. A spear-thrower or an archer also rode in the chariot. When the enemy came into range, they would launch their weapons. A chariot attack could panic the enemy, making them run from the battlefield.

Great Chariot Battle

In about 1274 BCE, the pharaoh Ramses II fought a great battle against the Hittites. It took place at Kadesh in present-day Syria. About 5-6,000 chariots were used in the battle, making it the largest chariot battle ever known. At first, it seemed the Hittites were winning, so the Egyptians panicked and started to run from the battle. Ramses stopped the panic and launched another attack on the Hittites, who then retreated into the city of Kadesh. Both sides claimed they had won, but the battle was probably a draw.

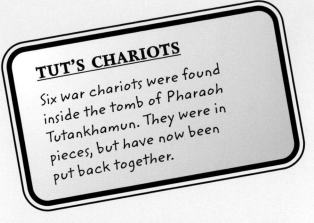

TUT'S CHARIOTS
Six war chariots were found inside the tomb of Pharaoh Tutankhamun. They were in pieces, but have now been put back together.

A dagger with a gold handle and its scabbard, or covering. The dagger belonged to Pharaoh Tutankhamun. The dagger and its scabbard were buried in the pharaoh's tomb when he died in 1327 BCE.

Writing

The ancient Egyptians believed that writing was a gift from the gods. This is why they called it *medu netjer*, which means "words of the gods." The Egyptians wrote with pictures called **hieroglyphs.** Each picture represented the sounds of words. We know much about ancient Egypt from hieroglyphs.

Hieroglyphs

In around 3100 BCE, hieroglyphs were invented and were then used for 3,500 years. Most ancient Egyptians could not read. Usually only nobles, royal people, and **scribes** were taught to read. Scribes were people whose job it was to read and write for the pharaoh or government.

This statue of a scribe shows him sitting cross-legged on the ground. He is writing on a papyrus sheet on his lap.

VERSATILE LANGUAGE

Hieroglyphs could be written from left to right, or from right to left. They could also be written in rows or in columns.

Tools

Scribes used pens and brushes to write, which they dipped in red or black ink. They wrote on sheets of **papyrus**, a type of paper made from a reed.

Hieroglyphs were also painted on the walls of tombs and carved in stone.

Spells to protect the dead were written in hieroglyphs on the walls of tombs.

Difficult Writing

Hieroglyphs were made up of hundreds of different signs, so it took a long time to write or read them. For everyday writing, scribes used signs that were easier and faster to write.

What Does it Tell Us?

When hieroglyphs died out, people forgot how to read them. No one knew what they meant until an incredible stone slab was found in Egypt in 1799. It became known as the Rosetta Stone, shown right. Carved on the stone was the same piece of writing in three different scripts—Greek, **demotic**, and hieroglyphs. Historians could read the Greek, so they compared that to the hieroglyphs. By doing so, they managed to understand them, and so could then start to read ancient Egyptian hieroglyphs.

Quiz

1. **Who had a "sidelock of youth"?**
   a. Boy children
   b. Men
   c. Women

2. **Who probably won the Battle of Kadesh?**
   a. Egyptians
   b. Hittites
   c. Neither—it was a draw

3. **What name did the ancient Egyptians give to their land?**
   a. Kemet
   b. Kermit
   c. Kismet

4. **What was a pyramid?**
   a. A tomb
   b. A temple
   c. A house

5. **Why is the Rosetta Stone important?**
   a. It listed every Egyptian pharaoh
   b. It helped people to read hieroglyphs
   c. It led to buried treasure

6. **What building material were houses made from?**
   a. Stone
   b. Wood
   c. Mud brick

7. **What was left inside the body of a mummy?**
   a. The brain
   b. The heart
   c. The lungs

8. **Which was the most important farm animal?**
   a. Sheep
   b. Cow
   c. Pig

9. **What was the punishment for tomb robbers?**
   a. To be whipped
   b. To be put in prison
   c. To be put to death

10. **Who was the god of the dead?**
    a. Anubis
    b. Hathor
    c. Osiris

ANSWERS

6. c.
7. b.
8. b.
9. c.
10. c.

1. a.
2. c.
3. a.
4. a.
5. b.

Timeline

c. 5500–3100 BCE A time in Egyptian history called the Predynastic Period, which was before Egypt had pharaohs.

c. 3100 BCE Upper Egypt and Lower Egypt were united to become one land. The first pharaoh, Narmer, came to power. Hieroglyphs were invented.

c. 2686–2181 BCE A time in Egyptian history called the Old Kingdom. Egypt was ruled by powerful pharaohs.

c. 2650 BCE Pharaoh Djoser built the Step Pyramid, the first pyramid.

c. 2560 BCE Pharaoh Khufu built the Great Pyramid.

c. 2181–2055 BCE A time in Egyptian history called the First Intermediate Period. Egypt was ruled by many minor pharaohs.

c. 2055–1650 BCE A time in Egyptian history called the Middle Kingdom. Egypt was ruled by powerful pharaohs.

c. 1650–1550 BCE A time in Egyptian history called the Second Intermediate Period. Egypt was ruled by foreign kings.

c. 1550–1069 BCE A time in Egyptian history called the New Kingdom. Egypt was at its most powerful. Pharaohs were buried in rock-cut tombs, not in pyramids. Expeditions were sent to foreign lands.

c. 1336 BCE Pharaoh Tutankhamun came to the throne.

c. 1274 BCE Pharaoh Ramses II defeated the Hittites.

c. 1069–715 BCE A time in Egyptian history called the Third Intermediate Period. A time of unrest. More than one pharaoh ruled at a time.

c. 747–332 BCE A time in Egyptian history called the Late Dynastic Period. Egypt was ruled by pharaohs from foreign lands.

332–30 BCE A time in Egyptian history called the Greco–Roman Period. Egypt was part of the Greek empire of Alexander the Great.

30 BCE Egypt becomes a province of the Roman Empire.

44–30 BCE Ptolemy XV Caesarion was the last pharaoh of Egypt.

Glossary

canopic jars The four jars that held the mummified stomach, liver, lungs, and intestines of a dead person.

capital A large city where a government or king lives and rules.

ceremonies Acts usually performed as part of a religious event.

current The flow of water in a stream, river, sea, or ocean.

demotic An ancient style of handwriting that could be written quickly.

fertile To be able to grow something, such as crops, easily.

goods Things that can be bought or sold, such as pots, food, and clothing.

government A group of people who help to run a country.

hieroglyphs The oldest writing used in ancient Egypt. It was made up of signs that stood for words and sounds.

intestines The internal organs found below the stomach.

linen The fabric made from the fibers of the flax plant.

mud brick Bricks made by mixing mud with water.

mummified To make a dead body into a mummy.

mummy An animal or human body preserved by drying.

nobles People who were thought to be more important than ordinary people.

papyrus A water reed used to make a type of writing paper.

precious metals Rare and valuable metals.

preserved To stop something from rotting.

prey The animals that are hunted and killed for food by another animal.

rushes Tall reeds that grow on the banks of a river.

scribe A person trained to read and write.

stonemason Someone who carves things from stone.

temple A building in which people worship a god or goddess.

worship To pray to and believe in a god.

Further Information

Books

How The Ancient Egyptians Lived
by Jane Shuter
(Gareth Stevens Publishing, 2010)

The Ancient Egyptians
by Lila Perl
(Children's Press, 2005)

The Ancient Egyptian World
by Eric H Cline and Jill Rubalcaba
(Oxford University Press USA, 2005)

Web Sites

Due to the changing nature of Internet links, PowerKids Press has developed an online list of Web sites related to the subject of this book. This site is updated regularly. Please use this link to access this list:
http://www.powerkidslinks.com/dig/egypt

Index

Akhenaten, King 13
Alexander the Great 28

canopic jars
clothing 12
crafts 12–13

death mask 15
Djoser 16, 28

embalmers 20, 21

farming 10–11
flooding 6, 10, 14
food 11

Giza 16, 17
government 14, 29

hair 12
Hatshepsut 15
hieroglyphs 24, 25, 28, 29
houses 8–9

Kemet 6
Khafre 17
Khufu 17, 28

Late Dynastic Period 28
Lower Egypt 7, 19, 28

makeup 12, 13
Memphis 7, 9
Menkaure 17
Middle Kingdom 28
mummification 15, 20–21, 29

Narmer, King 7, 28
Nefertiti, Queen 13
New Kingdom 28
Nile River 6, 7, 10, 14

Old Kingdom 28

papyrus 24, 29
pharaoh 7, 14–15, 16, 17, 22, 28
Ptolemy XV Caesarion 28
pyramids 16–17, 28

Ramses II 23, 28
religion 18–19
Roman Empire 28
Rosetta Stone 25

sphinx 14

temples 8, 9, 29
tomb robbers 16, 17
Tutankhamun 15, 23, 28

Upper Egypt 7, 19, 28

Valley of the Kings 7, 17
vizier 14

war 22–23
writing 24–25